Nature's Children

BLACK BEARS

Caroline Greenland

GROLIER
EDUCATIONAL

FACTS IN BRIEF

Classification of the Black Bear

    Class: *Mammalia* (mammals)
    Order: *Carnivora* (carnivores)
    Family: *Ursidae* (bear family)
    Genus: *Ursus*
    Species: *Ursus americanus*

World distribution.   Exclusive to North America. Related species widely distributed throughout most of the northern hemisphere.

Habitat.   Forest regions, swamps and dense bushland.

Distinctive physical characteristics.   Smallest of the North American bears; usually black with tan muzzle and white patch under throat; claws are comparatively short and curved.

Habits.   Primarily solitary; fast runner; skilled tree climber; sleeps deeply for most of the winter; wanders far for food.

Diet.   Plant life: roots, leaves, berries, grasses, fruit and acorns; small mammals, frogs, fish, insects; honey.

Published originally as
"Getting to Know . . . Nature's Children."

This series is approved and recommended by the Federation of Ontario Naturalists.

This library reinforced edition is available exclusively from:

GROLIER
EDUCATIONAL

Sherman Turnpike, Danbury, Connecticut 06816

Contents

Do you remember your very first Teddy Bear? It was probably soft and furry with little round ears, a black button nose and a squishy body just made for cuddling.

Children have had Teddies ever since the beginning of the century, when United States President Teddy Roosevelt saved a Black Bear cub from being killed. A toymaker, charmed by this story, decided that a bear would make a nice, huggable plaything for a child and created the first Teddy Bear.

Baby Black Bears look as huggable as toy Teddy Bears. But watch out! Their mother may be lurking nearby, ready to chase off anyone who comes near her babies.

These bears look cute and cuddly, but like all wild animals, they do not make good pets.

Bundles of Fun

Summertime is playtime for baby Black Bears. They chase butterflies, play tag and wrestle with each other, while their mother looks on.

If a hungry cougar or another bear comes too close, the mother shoos the cubs up the nearest tree. Then, growling fiercely, she scares off the intruder.

When the danger has passed, the mother calls to her babies, and they come shimmying down to the ground to play some more.

Once a cub is shooed up a tree by its mom, it may stay up for 20 hours or more until she says it's safe to come down again.

Black Bear

Brown Bear

Polar Bear

Bear Territory

Black Bears are the most common of the North American bears, and, compared to their relatives, the Brown and Polar Bears, they are also the smallest. Black Bears can be found across most of North America, up into Alaska and even as far south as Mexico. They prefer to live in thickly wooded areas or dense brushland, near a creek, stream or lake.

The Black Bears that live in North America have cousins in Asia. These Asiatic Black Bears are smaller than North American Black Bears and prefer to live in mountains and forests.

The Bear Facts

Male bears are also called boars. Black Bear boars weigh about 170 kilograms (375 pounds), which means it would take two fully grown men on one end of a teeter-totter to balance a Black Bear on the other end. Female bears, called sows, weigh slightly less than the males.

The shaded area shows where Black Bears are found.

Many-Colored Coat

Do not be fooled by their name. Not all Black Bears are black. Most are black with a brownish muzzle and a white throat patch or other white chest markings. But some Pacific Coast Black Bears are almost white; others are a bluish color. Cinnamon-colored Black Bears are quite common in Western Canada and the United States. In other areas, Black Bears may be brown, dark brown or even blue-black. Sometimes a mother will have cubs of different colors in the same litter, although this is unusual.

Whatever their color, all Black Bears have long, coarse fur that is not at all soft and cuddly like a Teddy Bear's coat. Every spring Black Bears shed their winter coat and grow a lighter-weight summer coat.

Scents, Sounds and Sights

The bear uses its long snout to sniff out other animals or a good supply of food, such as a patch of berries. To get a really big noseful of smells, a bear will often stand on its hind legs with its nose in the air.

A bear's rounded, furry ears are useful too. Its keen sense of hearing means it is difficult to sneak up on a bear without being noticed.

It is a good thing that a bear can smell and hear so well, because its eyesight is poor. In fact, a Black Bear has difficulty recognizing objects by sight. And Black Bears are color blind. This means they only see in shades of black, gray and white. They cannot see colors.

A Black Bear won't turn its nose up at very much. It will eat just about anything.

Bear Talk

If you overheard two Black Bears "talking," you would hear a strange combination of growls, whines and sniffs. Although you might have a problem understanding this "conversation," Black Bears do not. For instance, if a baby bear hears its mother making a sharp "woof-woof" sound, it knows danger is nearby. And every mother Black Bear knows that a baby-like cry means her young cub is in trouble—or hungry.

A bear often stands up to sniff the air for scents. It may even walk swaying its head from side to side, snuffling all the while.

Getting Around

Unlike many animals, but like you, bears put their whole foot, including their heel, on the ground when they walk. Because they do this with all four feet, they have an awkward, shambling walk. But if a bear is in a hurry, it can reach speeds of up to 55 kilometres (35 miles) per hour. A running bear looks a bit like a huge, black beachball bouncing through the woods.

Swimming is second nature to a Black Bear. It can "dog-paddle" across small lakes or rushing rivers with ease. When a Black Bear climbs out of the water it shakes itself dry like a big shaggy dog.

Black Bear paw prints

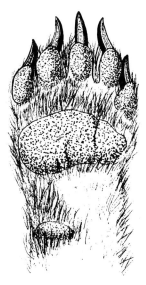

A bear usually travels along the same routes over and over again within its territory.

Front paw

Tree scratched by Black Bear

Opposite page:

The strong short claws of the Black Bear work much like grappling hooks when it is climbing a tree.

Going Up

If you were in a tree-climbing contest with a Black Bear, the bear would probably win. A Black Bear climbs trees to escape danger or to take a good look around for food. To help it climb it has five hooked claws on each paw. The bear hugs the trunk with its front paws and hooks its strong, curved claws into the bark. Then it pulls itself up with its front paws and pushes with its back paws. The bear does this so quickly that it looks as if it has leaped up the tree like an agile cat. But unlike cats, bears cannot pull in their claws. A bear's claws are always out and ready for action.

Coming Down

The Black Bear comes down the tree tail first, often dropping the last few metres (yards) to the ground. Although you might be shaken up by such a sudden landing, the Black Bear does not seem to even notice. It just picks itself up and ambles off into the underbrush.

Home Ground

Adult Black Bears keep out of each other's way most of the time. Each bear stakes out a territory that has enough food to keep it alive and healthy. In summer, when there are lots of green plants and berries, a bear's territory may be only three square kilometres (just over one square mile). But in spring, when plants are just beginning to grow and food is scarce, the bear's territory may be ten times as big.

A Black Bear warns other bears away from its territory by posting "Stay Out" warnings. To do this it stands on its hind legs beside a tree and claws the bark. Any bears that come along see these claw marks and know they are entering an area that belongs to another bear. They can even tell the size of the bear whose territory they have wandered into. How? The higher the claw marks, the bigger the bear.

Even this handy tree perch won't improve the view. That's because the Black Bear is very nearsighted. But its keen sense of smell and hearing more than make up for its poor eyesight.

Hungry as a Bear

When you think of a bear do you think of a ferocious meat-eating animal? Bears do eat meat, but they also eat plants. That is why they are called omnivores.

The Black Bear is not a picky eater. In fact, it will eat almost anything that is available. Most of its diet is made up of plants, roots, grains and fruit. The bear has very flexible lips and a long tongue which makes berry-picking easy. A bear's favorite fruits include blueberries, strawberries and apples. They also munch on nuts such as acorns, hazelnuts and beechnuts.

In spring, Black Bears that live near the coast dine on migrating salmon. A Black Bear will eat any meat it finds, but it will not normally kill another animal for food unless it is easy prey.

A Black Bear also loves honey, but did you know that it likes to eat bees too? Also high on its list of favorites are ants, grasshoppers, termites and wasps. A bear's thick coat helps protect it from being stung by angry wasps and bees.

Tough Teeth

To chew up all the different kinds of foods it eats, a Black Bear has different kinds of teeth. Sharp pointed meat-cutting teeth for catching prey are in the front of the bear's mouth. Broad flat cheek teeth called molars work like a potato masher to grind up tough plant fibers so the bear can digest them.

Opposite page:

The Black Bear, famous for its sweet tooth, often pokes its nose into tree hollows looking for honey.

Bears Alone and Together

During the summer and fall, a Black Bear is out from dusk to dawn searching for food and eating as much as possible. It needs to put on a good layer of fat in preparation for the long winter ahead when food is hard to find.

Summer is also the only time adult bears are likely to be seen together. That is because it is mating season. Once a bear finds a mate, the two spend a short time together—then they go their separate ways again!

Black Bears are usually loners, except in spring and summer when mom and babies often go down to the woods for a picnic of berries and other tasty treats.

Getting Ready for Winter

When the temperature falls and food becomes scarce, a Black Bear searches for a den in which to have its winter sleep. Finding a warm dry den is especially important for a mother Black Bear who is about to have a family. Long before the first snowfall she begins to inspect caves, hollow logs and overturned stumps for safety and dryness. Once she has chosen a spot, she covers the floor of her winter home with moss, leaves and grasses to make a warm nursery for her family.

Male bears are not nearly as fussy about their dens. They usually wait for the first snowfall before they even start looking for a den. By this time the females have moved into all the best spots. This does not seem to bother the male. If there is no den available, he simply lies down in the shelter of an overturned stump and waits for the snow to fall. As the snow piles up around him, his body warmth melts the snow closest to him, forming a custom-made igloo.

Opposite page:

Bears often gather dead leaves and grass and chewed off sticks as cozy bedding for their dens.

28

A Long Winter's Sleep

Black Bears in northern areas may nap for up to six months in winter. Bears from warmer regions, where food is available during the winter months, do not need to sleep for so long. Unlike true hibernators, a Black Bear may wake up and even leave its den if the weather is warm enough. When it gets cold again, the bear goes back to its den for another long snooze.

During this long winter's sleep the bear's breathing and heart rate slow down. This means that the bear needs less energy. Instead of having to eat food for energy, it can live on its stored fat.

When a Black Bear wakes up in the spring it is hungry and cranky and its stomach has shrunk because it has not eaten for so long. The first thing it does is look for food and water. Soon the bear's stomach will be full of new plant shoots and tree buds and the bear will be back to its roly-poly self.

Opposite page:

It doesn't matter if the berries are all gone, the bear will still eat the twig.

A Surprise for Mother.

Sows usually give birth to their tiny cubs in January or February, every other year. Mother bears in the north may be fast asleep in their snug dens when their babies are born. Just think of the surprise the mother bear gets when she wakes up and finds she is sharing her den with her new family!

Often there are two cubs, but sometimes there may be as many as five. Newborn Black Bear cubs are about the size of small squirrels. Their eyes are tightly shut, and they do not have any hair or teeth. They spend their first five weeks nursing and snuggling close to their mother's warm, furry body.

These cubs are probably between five and six weeks old. Their eyes are open and their newborn fuzz is being replaced by glossy fur.

Round and Round

When they first start to walk the small cubs have strong front legs and weak, wobbly back legs that they drag behind them. Young cubs cannot crawl in a straight line. Instead they usually go round and round in circles. This means they never get far away from their mother. That is a good thing, because the sow might be fast asleep and unable to keep an eye on them.

A cub gets its first look at the outside world when it is about three months old.

Padded Playground

When they are a week old, the cubs start to grow a fine coat of soft fur. They are able to see their mother for the first time at six weeks, but they are still very wobbly on their feet. Perhaps this is why they tend to spend their time climbing all over their mother, using her warm, furry body as a handy playground.

Bear School

The cubs are only puppy-sized when they leave the den for the first time in mid-April, so their mother keeps a close eye on them at all times. She is gentle and patient but quite strict with her cubs.

By watching their mother throughout their first year, the cubs learn all the skills a bear needs to survive: how to find the right kinds of food, how to look for shelter from bad weather, and what animals—such as cougars, lynxes, Grizzly Bears and adult Black Bears—to avoid.

Opposite page:

If this cub smiled, you might be able to see its milk teeth. Its permanent teeth won't start to grow in until it is nearly three months old.

Overleaf:

Two young cubs follow their mom across a beaver dam.

Weepy Wanderer

If a cub wanders off and gets lost, it cries and whines until its mother tracks it down. She then gently noses the wanderer back to the group. A crying cub is an upset cub; a contented cub purrs rather like a kitten.

When danger approaches the mother hustles the cubs up a tree for safety. But often the playful youngsters will climb trees just for the fun of it. They play tag with each other high in the trees and sunbathe on any convenient branch. In stormy weather, they take shelter in evergreen trees, using the overhanging branches as an umbrella to keep them dry.

Although bears are usually solitary creatures, sometimes two mother bears will travel together with their cubs. The females then share the task of cub-sitting, giving one of the mothers a chance to sleep or eat in peace.

It's amazing how small a branch a big Black Bear can stand on.

On Their Own

The cubs curl up in a den and sleep away the winter with their mother. Their survival lessons start up again in spring and continue until summer when the mother bear starts looking for another mate. At this point the yearlings, now as big as St. Bernard dogs, go on without their mother. However, they often stay with their brother or sister for the rest of the summer and may even share a den that winter.

The following spring, the cubs go their separate ways, putting their newly learned skills to the test. Strong bonds have developed between them, however, and if they meet later in their lives, they will be quite friendly toward each other.

Many trees have scars from the claws of the bears that have climbed them.

Put to the Test

The second year is the most difficult for a young Black Bear. Still small and inexperienced, it must find a territory with enough food to keep it healthy. And it must avoid larger bears, without the help of warning woofs from its mother. If it has learned its lessons well, a wild Black Bear will live to be ten or fifteen years old and have several families of its own.

Words to Know

Boar   A male bear.

Cub   Name for the young of various animals, including the Black Bear.

Den   Animal home.

Hibernation   Kind of heavy sleep that some animals take in the winter, during which their breathing and heart rates slow, and their body temperature goes down.

Hibernator   An animal that goes into hibernation for the winter.

Litter   Young animals born together.

Mate   To come together to produce young.

Molars   Broad flat cheek teeth that help grind up plant fibers.

Omnivore   An animal that eats plants and meat.

Sow   A female bear.

Territory   Area that an animal or group of animals lives in and often defends from other animals of the same kind.

INDEX

Photo Credits: Wayne Lankinen (Valan Photos), pages 4, 7, 13, 32, 38; Tim Fitzharris (First Light Associated Photographers), page 10; Norman Lightfoot (Eco-Art Productions), pages 14, 16, 37; T.W. Hall (Parks Canada), page 19; William Lowry (Lowry Photo), pages 20, 24, 29; Bill Ivy, page 23; V. Critch, page 27; J.D. Markou (Valan Photos), page 31; Hälle Flygare (Valan Photos), pages 34-35; Esther Schmidt (Valan Photos), pages 40-41, 42; Barry Ranford, page 45.

Printed and Bound in Italy by Lego SpA